Daybreak at the Straits and Other Poems

Also by Eric Ormsby

Araby

Facsimiles of Time: Essays on Poetry and Translation

For a Modest God: New & Selected Poems

Coastlines

Bavarian Shrine & Other Poems

Theodicy in Islamic Thought

Daybreak at the Straits and Other Poems

Eric Ormsby

Zoo Press

Zoo Press • P.O. Box 22990 • Lincoln, Nebraska 68542
Printed in the United States of America

Distributed to the trade by The University of Nebraska Press
Lincoln, Nebraska 68588 •www.nebraskapress.unl.edu

Cover design by Janice Clark of Good Studio © 2004
www.goodstudio.com

Library of Congress Cataloging-in-Publication Data

Ormsby, Eric L. (Eric Linn), 1941-
Daybreak at the straits and other poems / Eric Ormsby.
p. cm.
ISBN 1-932023-14-3 (alk. paper)
I. Title.
PS3565.R59 D39 2004
811'.54--dc22

2003022093

zoo023

First Edition

Acknowledgements

I thank the editors of the following journals in which certain of these poems first appeared:

Arc, Blueline, Books in Canada, Copia, Crux, Drunken Boat, The Fiddlehead, Gastronomica, Literary Imagination, Maison-neuve, The Malahat Review, Matrix, The New Criterion, The New Yorker, The New Quarterly, Parnassus and *Poetry Ireland Review.*

"Little Auguries" was first published as a broadside, in January 2003, by Delirium Press.

"The Song of the Whisk" first appeared in *The New Yorker*. It was subsequently set to music for two voices and piano by Jed Feuer and released on the CD *twenty-one songs* (Feuermusic, 2002).

"A Freshly Whitewashed Room" is forthcoming in the *The New Yorker.*

"Song for an Ironing Board" was set to music for soprano voice and piano by the composer Robin Attas and recorded in performance in 2003.

For my brother Alan

Table of Contents

III. Soliloquy at Nightfall in the Mayflower Hotel

The Jewel Box

I have not done with you, I have not done,
Dear Presences, who live on in the spun
braids of gold in the silk jewel box, who glance
at me from clumsy cameos, who dance
out of lurid corals or a split earring,
whose throats I summon to the supple string
where the oily pearls of buried evenings burn,
whose flesh I taste on my own lips in the sleek
surfaces of onyx or the bleak
bleared filigree some dutiful son brought back
from the gold-sellers' souk, the lightning-crack
in the brooch.

I have not done with your memories
who wreathe around me still, whose reveries
would smother me, dear loving vampires
whom imagination and my own desires
conjure out of gems and gold and paste.
Our ancestors are stronger than the taste
of some abandoned attar we still find
back of the jewel box where sweet shadows wind
remembrance out of fragrance until our tongues
burn like the first air breathed into newborn lungs.

I

Daybreak at the Straits

What the Snow Was Not

The snow was not liver-spotted like a gambler's
Hands. It did not reflect
Violet abrasions at the hubs of wheels
Or the well-glossed ankles of policemen.

The snow did not mimic flamingo rookeries
Or bone-stark branches where the spoonbills nest.
It had no single tint when it negated gold.
The snow was not duplicitous like arc

Lamps at sunrise that encairn the curbs
In lavender melodics. Snow did not web
The hands of women with their sudden hair
Electric-trellised in a blue downdraft.

The snow did not consume the eager mouths
Of children. It did not inhabit the skimming owl's
Concavity of surveillance and it did not flock
In grackle-shadows near the eaves of courts.

When you endow the snow with what it's not
—mere shivering crystals blown by January
over the squares in frosty negatives—
the snow becomes a god and nothing's lord.

Another Thing

To live in the body like a nervous guest;
To be confined in fingers and in feet;
To swing on the pendulum of what to eat;
To be subject to south and east and west . . .

Behind my skullbone lives another thing
That fidgets anxiously as I barge by,
That swivels skyward its chameleon eye
For the interest in the twitches of a wing.

My inmost dweller is predacious root;
Ransacks reality for steadfastness;
Adores the constancy of all dark stars;
Refuses thirst and thrives upon the brute
Benedictions of the wolf and lioness;
Loves the futility of fountains; preens scars.

Ant-Lion

Beneath your shoe soles an illusion smooths
the loose lank sandgrains into cavities
so exquisitely cocked that if you tease
their edges with a straw the funnel seethes

suddenly under to blank avalanche.
I saw a plodding ant's insouciance
topple it over in a scramble-dance
down down down into the clench

of the ant-lion, Chaplinesque
assassin of the sand, snug predator,
larval hunter with a gladiator
lunge of needle-mandibles, burlesque

Doodlebug, we called it, to domesticate
terror made tiny, mayhem minusculed.
Below our eyes its drab precision ruled
Lilliputian worlds with silicate

strategies, glint-façades of fright;
and sometimes when the ambushed day
bleedingly withdrew to slumbrous gray,
I heard my heartbeat striking in the night.

In dream sometimes the cliff-brink of the world,
that zigzag fracture of hurt porcelain
that leads beyond the darkness of the brain,
funnels and shimmies, woozies to a hurled

helterskelter of ankles and shrill clothes
upended, and we paw, in a fierce crawl,
bare air, eyes dragged upward as our bodies fall,
somersaulted, with heart-stoppered mouths.

And if our fall were only infinite,
if falling were our pleasure and our grace,
if our momentum obviated place,
if our descent were indeterminate . . . !

What taloned nightmare grips us in the wild
spiral of sleep? What ripped awakening?
What busy, greedy, inconspicuous thing?
What barely fledged phantasm of a child?

The ant-lion shrugs aside its camouflage,
ruthless as a consumer elbows near
with upraised boning knife to shear
something for that deep-freeze in the garage.

In dream we flutter above everyone.
In dream we Ixion the darkened sun.
Under our shoes a pinch of sand holds night
—darkness puppeteered by appetite.

Dicie Fletcher

Whene'er, along the ivory disks, are seen,
The filthy footsteps of the dark gangrene;
When caries comes, with stealthy pace to throw
Corrosive ink spots on those banks of snow–
Brook no delay, ye trembling, suffering fair,
But fly for refuge to the dentist's care . . .

—Solyman Brown, *Dentologia: A Poem on the Diseases of the Teeth* (1833), Canto 4

Πεῖρεν 'οόδόντων

—Iliad xvi, 405.

"I have a horror of unconsciousness," she said.
She refused the nitrous oxide mixed with oxygen
(that still was new in 1881).
"Let me come clear-eyed unto Calvary,"
Dicie Fletcher, teacher of Classics, said,
hands braced against chintz armrests while she watched
Dr. Diore's lancing eye,
cool blue sun in incandescent sky,
assay each tooth-tap as he inch-
wormed nearer, nearer and still
nearer to that secret place
where her sick tooth pulsed with pain.

"Would you reduce me to the mere *insensible*,"
she remembered, now, to her horror, having said.
"I tell you this, I disapprove of all
nepenthe. True propriety
must objurgate Lethean balm."
O now, how she cursed those cool
Ciceronian cadences of hers!

The bad tooth
seemed to flinch back like a guilty thing.
"They do some tiptop things these days
with hippopotamus," Dr. Diore drawled.
"It's all the thing—*ivory swaged with gold!*"
He saw the same old Dicie he had known
and hankered for for years. Since grammar school.

He shivered picturing her virginal
pale flesh swaddled inside stays and straps,
a woman barricaded behind her clothes.
(And was he not the man to lay her siege?)
And Dicie looked at him, saw him up close.
His muttonchops were snarled with bloody flecks.
His jowl was peppered with old smallpox pits.
She remembered him as a small and shiftless boy,
—now he'd got an office of his own, now
his thick and stubby fingers reeked of clove.

Her neckveins pounded and her temples rang.
And when Dr. Diore touched the culprit tooth
she writhed against the brimming of the hurt
that wrung out fiery teardrops from her eyes.
The Cross, Oh the Crown of Thorns . . .
faded from her, faded!

. . . peiren odonton . . .

Homer was the true Evangelist
—that's what she taught her boys.
Homer did not assuage, met doom
head-on. Uncoddled by all gospels he
only held out hard pebble-phrases for
the agonized to suck. Yes, *peiren: drove*
(aorist, boys? Who can tell me about this verb?
"Patroclus *drove* the spear *between the teeth*
—*odonton*—of Thestor, son of Enops. He
gaffed the charioteer out of his chariot
like a bullfrog on a pole.") The doctor
whooped, "We've got it now!" (Genitive
plural, that *ômega*, boys, Homer's own
words—chilly as ivory, aloof to pain.)
She felt the bulldog bite of the clamp.
She moaned and Dr. Diore stroked her brow.
"O my, my, yes, the *torture of the forceps*," he consoled.
(O how he wanted this woman, wanted her now!)

When a dark oak is cracked by cyclonic wind
and its lashed branches flail in the shrill black air
and the whole of heaven eddies with laceration
while under the skreegh of wind the herdsman hears
acorns pittering the rain-pocked soil
with palpitant volleys, gatling-gravel-pings,
so Dicie heard, from deep inside her skull,
how the tormenting third molar grunted, squeaked,
then twitter-stumbled like a stub of chalk
scraped across a blackboard to a shriek,
and she blubbered as the thick-embedded roots
tore at her gums till all at once,
with a popping suck it clopped into the dish
and rattled there, long-rooted, flung to defeat,
like Thestor when the quick
Patroclus hooked him down to black
Acheron and the terrible darkness came upon his eyes.
"Some alveolar mutilation . . . ," droned the doc.
(Tenderly his left hand brushed her throat.)

The cruelty of remembered Greek
came to her help. Grammar, that
propriety of all well-measured speech,
comforted even the mouth too torn to speak.
Didn't our Lord cry out on Golgotha?
Only language stood against
the unimaginable savagery
of gods unable to imagine pain.

"Your courage . . . extraordinary," mumbled Diore.
He thought of inviting Dicie for a sleigh-ride,
he bent to kiss her hand but she,
she dismissed him, cowed him, with a curt
inclination. Shaking, she gathered up
her reticule. She smoothed her bloody skirt.
She would not loose a cry for all the world
though her whole body howl. She swayed,
struggled to say "I thank you, Doctor," but
it came out thickly as *Ah fank yu, Dagga . . .*

(Hopelessly, aflame with lust he stood . . .)
True, in her pain she'd longed to roar
You base tooth-carpenter! and damn his eyes;
but this would have been ignoble, *infra dig*,
utterly at variance with what's decorous.
The doctor bowed and she bowed back to him.
I'd rather die than let
my suffering occasion a discourtesy.
What would we mortals be without propriety?
Swoopingly he held the door for her.

Precarious in hero as in suffragette,
propriety is terror turned to etiquette.

A Fragrance of Time

1

Time is not sequential but serpentine.
Time winds in retrogressive coils.
Time monuments itself in sudden pearls,
accretes and crests and columns travertine
confections that turn vaporous as lace.

Time has a cabalistic face
with inward-starring facets, stalagmites
as delicate as dials;
vials
of stoppered venom;
malachites
of moments gone awry,
Gehenna's timetables, and the sly
motherboard where all the minutes die.

Time with its plenum
panoply—oh *la durée*!
The secondhand is scintillant in disarray.

2

For us death's moment will be crystalline,
the vein of quartz within the lode of time,
and promise of the ores of consequence.
I who have always cherished sentience
the way the May-wind-ruffled columbine
cradles its petals as its leafstalks climb,
am privileged to know that moment mine.

Cessation is itself a fragrance of time.

A Salt Marsh near Truro

The wind has rubbed the dead trees to a shine
and now it flattens all the grasses down
to cowering bundles, slick and serpentine,
that twist and curtsey by the muddy brown
brink of the salt marsh with its alkaline
tinctures that transfigure what they drown.
The trees form a writhy circle with their brine-
burnt branches hooked up like the six points on a crown.

Gnats and midges, the fumes of raw methane,
that oily sun going down along the Bay
veiled in bright pollutants, and the wind
eroding everything to its low plane,
convince you that this marsh of hot decay
leaves nothing newborn that has not been skinned.

Two Views of My Grandfather's Courting Letters

Quidve mali fuerat nobis non esse creatis?
—Lucretius

1

So here is where it all began, in these
limp prevarications and apologies!
I recognize Grandfather's courting voice too well,
its little stylistic flinches: "It would be swell
if you held me still *Your Affectionate Friend . . .* "
he coaxes and then, abjectly, near the end,
"Don't judge me so hard, Miss Juliet, despite
the jackass I made of myself last Saturday night."

I could be reading letters I wrote myself,
except that these have lain 94 years on a shelf.
These are his courtship letters, which she saved,
locked in a metal strongbox, though she raved
against his "great foolishness" all her long old age.
She kept his memory bright in the soft claw of her rage.

Reading these letters I want to shout:
"Grandfather, stop! Fold up the paper. Switch out
the lamp on the supper table. Put back the quill
pen, whittled to a nib, in its snug inkwell
and tuck the unfranked stamps in the escritoire.
Cross your wedding date from the calendar.
Sidestep the meager pleasures, the great pains, to come
—the horror of a wedding bed that left you numb,
the brusque rebuffs or, at best, the grudged embrace
in conjugal obligation to prolong the human race.
I beg of you, I, wiser by nothing but distance,
confer on us, out of your countrified extravagance
and gentle hospitality
(my single memory of you,
kind whiskers and a kiss),
confer on us,
with what you fail to write,
the pure gift: not to be."

2

Holding his old letters I can see
how he copied each word out painstakingly
—a schoolboy polishing his copperplate.
All his hopes are still inviolate.
And I would not have it otherwise at last.
I would not soften the horror of the past.
But see, between the salvaged paragraphs,
the clumsy jauntiness, the staves and staffs,
laborious penmanship, with curlicues,
affected, to impress and to amuse.

The penning of these letters on the page
fissures the time between, a saxifrage
stubbornness of promise. I have seen the root
pierce rock. I have seen the puny shoot
split stone where it flowers and endure.
Not-being-born appears so pure
but my grandfather's clumsy courtliness
shyly jollies nothingness,
embarrasses as it redeems.
I fold his letters back along their seams
and shelter them in sandalwood.

And I will say, *Write us in the book of life,*
Grandfather, inscribe us there for good.

In the Abrahamic lamp
of a Georgia twilight, my grandfather picks up his pen
and writes,

Dearest Juliet,

Will you be mine?

Cremains

I dread the furnaces whose flickers turn
the citrine tincture of a tourmaline
and flack and deckle you the way gangrene
envenoms flesh with lustres of an urn.

Cremains is not a pretty word. You burn
to little clinkers with acetylene
spigots of combustion that careen
and scorch and roar till no one can discern

your earlobe from your Adam's apple or
your coccyx or your clavicle, your
left nut from your right, your nipple or
your uvula. Baby, you'll cook till you're
a soup-dish full of cinders which they'll pan
punctiliously, then pour into a can.

Little Auguries

The vast summer's distillate of cloud
rambled, thunder-proud,

while monuments of wind
bereaved my lips and left the bramble skinned.

The friendship of the ant instructed me,
I knew the honeybee's buzz-brevity.

Saluting thistles sentinelled the road:
I studied Numbers with a speckled toad.

I was tower-intoxicated, spire-
elated, the acolyte of mire-

rubies, pinnacles, abysses, mines;
what dusky zenith eglantines

Bacchic arbors of white mulberries
where patient worms, Penelopes

of satin, tend decennial looms.
I locked my summer in their silken rooms.

Expectancies of cumulus and shadowy
prefigurations of what memory

inhabited my ignorance?
An inconspicuous magnificence

swanned in the spotted sink
or lipped the spigot where I stole a drink

or crested the gold bristles of my manhood
or nestled in my nipple where the blood

pattered like storm-drops at my sullen skin,
entreating each least clod to let me in.

I knew the rivulets of Georgia clay,
their ripe persimmon ochres, their cachet

catastrophe inscribed in crevices,
nettled my reveries, and cornices

of sandlots, stinkpot pools;
the magnesium of mackerel schools

kindled the scuffed canal
with incandescences of protocol.

Out of frogspawn, oil-irises,
cavalcades unwound. The circuses

of polliwogs and the eyeless newt,
polka-dotted like a wind-stunned fruit,

spelled out the alphabet of wonder.
I suffered to the tutelage of thunder.

Mrs. Lazarus

Believe me, it isn't easy
even in a king-size bed
to sleep with the living dead.
You think I can enjoy
buttering his morning toast
when the butter's not so cold as his gray ghost?
And he's always so theatrical:
"Honey, what I've been through!"
I say, "Be a little stoical.
You could be lying in that sleazy
mausoleum. Instead, you're here. With me."

And let me tell you straight,
it's no mean trick to stimulate
a man like that
fresh from a grimy grave:
he needs a paramedic just to shave.
At night his chilly skin
sweats like a ripening cheese
and little bits keep dropping off
till the poor guy's scared to sneeze.
And the pills, the specialists, the life supports!
There's even Streptomycin in his shorts.

I don't like the way he sits and squints
or tilts off to one side in his La-Z-Boy.
Wouldn't you think he'd have a few small hints
for the living? Instead he whimpers *Ach!* or *Oy!*
"Honey," is all he says, "it wasn't Vegas!"
All night I smell his interrupted death.

It's my own individual hell.
All night I hug his contagious
carcass dripping with verminous breath.
I calm him as he dreams and squirms.

I who adore Chanel
now lie down with worms.

Cradle-Song of the Emperor Penguins

Shackleton is stranded far to the north of us,
the *Endurance* stands gripped in the fists of the ice.

The skuas have withdrawn to the cape, the leopard
seals laze in the sun of the Weddell Sea.

Our wives have trekked back to warm surf having laid
their eggs on our feet to brood-hatch with our blood.

Our empresses have left us to the long night of the ice
—like goalies we cradle tense futures on our toes,

dandling our babes against our belly skin:
all winter we shall stand in a pod of palaver

against the winds of Erebus and shield our chicks
under pouches of down and coverlets of quill.

In the long night of the world when the green
krakens of the aurora writhe

we fast and hold our hunger to the wind.
Our children hatch darkly. They hug our toes for life.

My tufty chicks, my fuzz-downy bairns,
I will guard you when the leopards

of September return. I will shield you
when the towers topple into the seas of ash.

The soot of winter night is on my tongue,
the cinder of ambushed dawn is in my eyes,

yet I will shelter you against my belly-skin
and warm your feather-weakness with heart's blood
and cradle you on the crèches of my claws.

Rowing into the Glades

I had pledged myself to rescue princesses
from the paws of ogres. I had held my sword
between my eyes and made a solemn vow,
like Galahad or Lancelot,
and Tommy, bold as me, had sworn the same.

Now, with sunburnt shoulders, in a seethe
of weeds, with griping oarlocks, we
angled our rowboat up the drainage creek.
We were following the levee engineers
had mounded high against the rivulets
Okeechobee brims before it spills
and sidles toward the Gulf in whispering
tributaries, lost to sight.

A kite mewed. We heard the plash
mud turtles made careening from a log.
A water beetle surfed the troughs we carved.
The creek was deep, the water dark as tar.
The sun, sadistic princeling on a counterpane
of plush thunderheads, squinted fierily down
and seared the lowly grasses of the shore.

Beyond a crook in the coiling stream we heard
what sounded like a woman's voice in pain.
Our princess? Tommy bent to his oar-stroke,
I redoubled mine and so
we fairly scooted ourselves around the bend.

Ahead of us in a flurry of beating wings
a marsh hen was shrieking as it fought to fly.
We oared the rowboat closer, gingerly.
"She's caught beneath," said Tommy, then,
as I dragged the bird out, "*Jesus H. Christ!*" he yelled.
A snapping turtle hung from the broken leg
and was working its beak to drag the marsh hen down
with snake-like twitches of its hook-shaped head.
"He won't let go till it thunders," Tommy said.

I opened my hand, the bird slid under,
In sudden stillness we could hear the creek
crawl along the bottom of our hull. We
listened for the water as it drew
twigs and leaves and weeds and feathers down.

We heard it suck at the muddy banks and lap
the roots of saw grass and of bayberry.
And in the water was another sky
with a lone sun and its companion clouds
in serpentine reflections by our prow.
The black creek had swallowed all it saw.

That was the way it was for both of us
before the world began.
Now we understood, with open eyes,
how the deeps are always dragging down what flies.

White Phalaenopsis

The protocol of orchids lies in subterfuge:
swanning petals form a curve's cortege
where slant diplomacies of lip engage

the winter-dociled bee. Such grace is made
of tasseled rhetoric, arced only to dissuade:
See how the orchid angles out of the white shade

that shrouds its calyx. Form can never lie,
we tell ourselves, although the pilgrim fly
find heaven in fragrance where it comes to die.

Is the orchid's flowering but stratagem,
mere disillusion of a diadem,
or our most shadowy Elysium?

Childhood Pieties

I grew up sullen, nervous, full of tricks.
St. Paul and Milton were familiar ghosts.
I sniffed First Disobedience from the bricks
and mildewed plaster of the Lord of Hosts;
from smiling lies rouged with a crucifix;
the naphtha'd parlour and the sabbath roasts;
the bitter bibles where the saved would mix
apocalyptic gossip with their boasts.

I smirked rebellion and wet my bed.
Even the lustre of their sheets was fraud.
At nightmare time their Saviour, leeched with sin,
crept in beside me, worming through my head,
embraced me, stroked me, kissed me while I clawed
the frogcold mouth of jesus on my skin.

Daybreak at the Straits

For Richard Outram

1

The clouds that lie in cinnabar striations
are juggled by a nimble waterspout
too distant for significance. The dim
pink of daybreak binds the sky with dark
barely distinguishable from a darker sea.
The horizon mortices itself with chinks of rose.
What we call day is nothing more
than disintegrated darkness at the Straits.
Night bickers for asylum still
in unlaced shoes, implores the paling windowpanes
to be steadfast for dark against the light.
I am witness to the spectral provocations
daylight introduces to a vista
that all night stood
islanded by nothing but the stars.

2

Tired of the meditations on futility
that now retard my nights I walked to see
the waters of the Straits in darkness hesitate,
recoil and hover, tremble just before they calibrate
shocked sandstone, the staved cliff, the pitiable
barricades we raise against the terrible
erosions waves exact. The wind's a whittler here,
pares quartz to thinnest splinters, loves the sheer
spare sea-lathed skeletons of objects cast ashore.

It comforts me at night, a watchman of the stars
that only change by reasonable laws, to parse
the luminous degradations of the dark
as lethal light insinuates and tinges. Dogs bark
down at Rice Point, a rooster clears its throat outside.
From the cliff a cormorant topples like a suicide.

3

In the watches of the night, as the Psalmist said,
I meditate on darkness, I remember my dead.
The dark is palpable, has a silken-sash-drawn feel,
gloves the troubled fingertips with a cochineal
comfort, the way spring water laves the skin
with its brisk plush touch. I will gather in
my hours as the darkness climbs and spreads.
It has become the ocean. Up to our heads
we bob and drift, remembranceless,
and for all we cling to spars of nothingness,
names burn their starlight on dark irises.

I feel the soul inside me, dear dieresis
that thews my breath and flesh, that separates
heart's thrusting muscle as it meditates
from all the rough heart cherishes, I sense
the supple disjunctions of the animal
threshed in the indiscernible
meshes of the element and, terrified,
crow with the cock and bark with the farmer's dog,
wriggle awake, crawl from the salt bog
of sleep unsatisfied:

on my lips and on my eyelids as the new
sun shoulders the clouds aside,
a darkness sits, intangible as dew.

A Freshly Whitewashed Room

I am sitting in the bedroom where Grandmother
Entered Calvary, where her halting breath
Finagled the stiff-laced curtains to puff out.
I am in the sunny bedroom where she lay
So long ago, tortoised in a cast
From chin to groin. How the pallid sweat
Fled from her flesh and smarted, made her
Itch with agony while I would read
The Life of Stonewall Jackson in a high
Annunciatory voice. Unknowingly I was
Her tongue of doom. The downfall of the South
Was in her bandaged bones where Stonewall bled
Tragical as Hector although not
Heel-dragged around the city gates
But fusilladed by his own smoke-staggered men.

And she would sweat and blink in the lamp
Near where I'm sitting now, though
Early sunshine pours in from the east
And the walls are freshly whitewashed
Till they fairly blaze.
Is there a sickroom sweetness just behind this new
White wall, a troubled coughing in the wainscoting
Where field-mice cache their stores? Are there echoes
Of her outcries in the dismantled fixtures?

Sometimes I think the sufferings of the old
Make heroes look ridiculous.
Sometimes I think to bring down Ilion
Was simpler than to guide the bitter spoon
At medicine time to the reluctant lip.

And when the heavy book sagged in my hands
And I would nod off in the bedside chair,
"Honey," she'd say to me, "go over that page once more.
I need the fortitude of good example now."
Each caisson-jolt and bivouac emboldened her.
She grappled her pain like an antagonist.

Yet, when I read out loud to her,
It felt as if my voice
Were wearing her away
And inching her into that history
She always so clamored for.
With every word I read she seemed to me
Some punished stone an ocean worked upon,
Lapping around her till it covered her
Down to the bare bedrock it rubbed away.

II

Domestic Questions

Watchdog and Rooster

Surveying the henhouse with profound
vigilance, taut on his tether,
alert in sleet as well as heatstroke weather,
crouched, eye ajar, the farmer's hound.
The rooster, however,
accustomed to the chuckling palaver
of his cackleophilous concubines,
disliked the stolid silence of the dog
who hunched there like a stinkpot on a log
and only uttered small, obsequious whines
about his master's boots at supper-time.

Let us see (the rooster mused) *if this dull mutt,*
this grovel-muzzled mongrel, this bacon-butt,
this caravan of fleas, this tick-parade,
this yap-infested bozo, slow and spayed,
let's see, I say, if this back-alley terrier,
this rumple-bellied harrier
of shrews and voles, of polecats and hedgehogs,
can cut the mustard with the bigger dogs!

Rooster waited till the dog, galvanized
by gazing, nodded; then, in fowlish pantomime
he stalked across the barnyard in a trot
until he reached a strategic spot
below the watchdog's downward drooping ear.
He then let fly a loud chantecleer
rawp that left the stunned hound paralyzed.
The hound had never been hard
of hearing, quite the opposite.
The clangorous crowing of the rooster, shrill pasha,
rattled in his brainpan like a washer
on a wind-tormented pipe. He pounced.
He took the raucous rooster by the throat and trounced
him on the barnyard till he bit
his insupportable windpipe cleanly through.

The moral of this fable still rings true:
Muzzle the watchdog when you cock-a-doodle-doo.

Episode with a Potato

I was skinning a potato when it said:
Please do not gouge my one remaining eye!
My parer hesitated. The knob of the spud
comforted my hand-hold with its sly
ovoid, firm yet brittle as a fontanelle,
and I much enjoyed the way its cool lump
—all pulpy planes and facettings, with a starch
sheen that mildly slimed my fingers
(not to mention that tuberous smell
that lingers
like the shoulder of a clump
of creosote bushes or the violet mildew of an arch
no triumph still remembers)
—yes, I liked the way it occupied my pinch.

I understood at its tiny squeak
the power of pashas over the members
of their entourages. For a week,
whenever I passed, the potato would flinch.
Its one eye never slept.
I thought of the kingdoms it had crept
through under the ground, spud-
smug, amid the dust of the bones of shahs
and eunuchs, those generations of the Flood,
the Colossi and the Accursed,
the Great Hunger and the hegiras,
telemons and ostraca and worst,
immense anti-archives of dirt.

It hurt
me to do it but I scooped out its eye
and ate it and felt utterly triumphant: I
ingested all that a potato could personify.

Song for an Ironing Board

I ride an ironing board to reach the stars.
I prick it with my spurs of spatulas.
It neighs and ripples the old scorch-scars
of its back and flanks. It whinnies,
and I rear back, snorting steam.
I bridle my ironing board with wrinkled bras.
I rein it in with underwear.
How it stamps and paws its trestle!

O many's
the dawn I've ridden forth with the gleam
of a fresh-pressed collar and jousted with legions
of wrinkles and mutinous pleats.
The unstarched world's Cimmerian regions
yield to my singeing hoof-beats.

I ride an ironing board to reach the heights
beyond all rumpledoms of wrinkled wash
where the shirtwaist alone shines triumphant.
I ride an ironing board as the iron's lights
like clangorous horse-shoes knicker and clip.
I ride an ironing board that gallops to my lash.
It rears like Hannibal's last elephant,
Alp-traumatized, and trumpets. Its fireproof lip
psalmodizes—
O my war-stallion, snort-eloquent!

The Song of the Whisk

My flail demolishes
the gold of yolks;
my mesh abolishes
what it would coax.

The waterspout can frisk
while it soufflés the sea;
what's the twister but a whisk
for instant entropy?

I will erect a pinnacle
of undulant bearnaise;
with clicketing quite clinical,
paradisal mayonnaise.

Domestic Questions

Sometimes during supper when my wife
cried like a parrot tethered to a perch
I used to ask, Why should she suffer so?
Why should her pearly scales display
the calcium of sadness quite so sandily?
Why should her nicked and nibbled beak
struggle to contain her agile tongue?
Why should my madness be her private perch
where she strops her beak and sequin-silly claws
like a manicurist flicking out a damp stale towel?
Why should my horror be the cage where she
nestles down at night beneath the hood,
hearing beyond the darkness of my mind
the friendship of some far-off radio
or those noises people utter when they think
they're all alone, those chippy clicks
they make by tapping their thumbnails on their teeth?
Why should she huddle like a wing-clipped bird,
some lorikeet, some hyacinthine thing,
budgerigar puffed up on cuttlebone
bunching blue after-feathers against the frost?

Time as Escargot

Suppose time were not spirally and filigreed
but rather went
ambling more randomly. Imagine
time as *escargot*, as succulence
with all remembrance curved
concentrically inside a patterned shell,
thick toward the middle then more tenuous
as newer chambers belly out above;
that is, not cyclical but
diatoming inward on itself, a
pulsing palimpsest of the ever old
configured as the new:

O Snail,
the sexual residue you leave on dials,
on watch-crystals and on grandfather clocks,
your glistening viscosities of time,
your sweet slime,
patina instants, all
heirloomed in a chiton's curl.

Vacuum Pantoum

The vacuum's cannistered voracity
never gets enough; its gulf-presidium
snootsavors carpet, its mumbo-continuum
snuffles triple-ply with toothed tenacity.

I overhear the siren in the vacuum
bag that serenades as it asseverates
lint-detritus or evacuates
the peregrine residuum

that effloresces on my velveteen.
The mites in their minute imperium
are obliviated by this wolf-harmonium
whose howl's Aeolian and gabardine.

O hoover me! I hear sprawled sofas hum,
Suck on my pleats! the buxom curtains plead.
The kilim pimps the nozzle for a knead.
The louvers quiver for the slot-scoop's thumb.

The Gorgon in the Urn

I keep the family gorgon in the urn.
I don't parade it on the mantelpiece.
I keep it in the pantry behind a fern,
Swaddled by a verdigris of bacon grease.

My gorgon likes to tap against the lid
And shake her cage when I have company.
If any lady says, *Medusa me*,
I hold my urn against her carotid.

O gorgon I have urned, my gorgonette!
O clasp of adders writhing and tentacular!
Visage that incinerates the synapses!

I love the sensual ciphers of her sweat
That beads upon her bronze as it collapses.
I love the lashes of her coiled vernacular!

A Dachshund in Bohemia

For Hugíček

The bristle-pelted Nimrod of the rat,
snout-partisan
of passageways and mildewed catacombs,
aroma-artisan,
more slink-insinuating than the barnyard cat,
the badger hound homes
in on ferrets and on errant mice.
He scruffs them in the vise

of his unmerciful mouth and swags
them by their neckbones back and forth,
slack gobbets
of fur they dangle from *jezevčík's* snout.
The brillo-coated *chlapec*
brags
for all his yapping triumph's worth
and rasps the doorjamb till he's ushered out.

The low-slung hammock-belly of this hound
grazes the ground.
His swizzle-brush of tail tattoos
Sousa marches when he's agitated.
It does not amuse
the long-haired dachshund to be equated
with taller dogs:
They seem precariously inflated
to our gruff terrier who completely wags
from muzzle to tail-tip when appreciated.

Jezevčík : Dachshund (in Czech)
chlapec: fellow, guy

An Epistle from Rice Point

Nothing's gone smoothly at Rice Point. The cod
I cooked for lunch the other day had worms
and when I forked the fillet gingerly,
a fat and pinkish snout came writhing out.
My sons were sickened and quite off their feed
but I addressed the impertinence of squirms
that had enlaced our lunch, with three
brusque dollops of hot sauce. It flailed about
and finally it spoke, that worm, and said,
How dare you ladle sauce upon my head?
I am the abyssal worm that feeds
in darkness on the deep floor of the sea
—a tender coiling consciousness that breeds
in the fibers of the flesh, a wriggle-god,
a lithe mind that rivulets stupidity—
the lumpy and dull-witted race of cod . . .

"The cod was beautiful, and you are not,
you slimy eyeless annulated pest,"
I shot back and I brained it with a pot.
The worm came eeling back and now addressed
my dumbstruck sons:

At midnight I will twist
all through your nightmares, I'm the worm
the Gospel speaks of that will never die,
and I dwell with the worm that dieth not
inside your brainpans like a doubled fist.
Behind your foreheads where the bad dreams squirm,
I'll snuggle up and peek out through your eye,
unless you eat me live.

I took the hot
tip of my carving knife and chopped the talkative beast
in sections, but each inch curled and writhed,
a dozen cod-worms down the platter scythed
in a sort of Todestanz combined with jive.

We are the laily worms that haunt the sea,
the wormy segments piped in harmony.
We are envenomed with the dreams of reefs,
the lobsters' anxieties, the oysters' griefs,
the lachrymose neurosis of the eel,
the torpid Weltschmerz *of the cochineal . . .*

"Enough!" I thundered and switched on the Moulinex,
"I've had enough of this annelid hex!"
I sluiced the worm-ends in the cannister,
set it to *Mince* and then *Puree*, but faster
than I could macerate those vocal segments
their shrill harmonics rang in yammer fragments.
A soup of cod-worms gave a grand chorale
from the kitchen at Rice Point. My terrified
teenagers watched the worm broth swell
tentacular and spittle-crested, a pale pink tide
of liquid parasitic cod-worm consommé
engulfed us where we crouched. I cried, *Assez!*
We wolfed the worm-soup down with zealous spoons
and mopped up every drop. The taunting tunes
have ended now for good. All is again well
here by the ocean at Rice Point.
Farewell . . . Farewell.

Our Spiders

(*Naši pavouci . . .*)

Our spiders are theatrical.
Their webs are glitzy and their spinnerets
sequin the silks they unspool as they spin.
They step processional as majorettes,
each pedipalp held firm against each shin,
their swivel-eyes fur-bristled and octagonal.

Our spiders are most musical:
Their eight silk-glands echo calliopes
that pedal, as they strum their tender strings,
chromatic and Minervan melodies
that quiver on the hornet's captive wings
like Palestrina at his most polyphonal.

Our spiders are convivial,
with intersecting webs of bonhomie;
they pool the vagaries of katydids,
they interlace to ward off anomie;
and when an aging spider hits the skids,
she's invited to a brunch that's terminal.

Some say our spiders are maniacal;
that paranoia complicates their orbs;
that mutterings among them multiply
and that they snare each other with veiled barbs;
that the trapdoor spider gorged on caddis fly
considers the tarantula fanatical.

I say our spiders are rhapsodical
eremites of tactile syllables.
They weave a sisterhood where vocal silk
labyrinths their mystic mandibles.
Gorgias must have sipped a spider's milk.
Like him they shimmer-loom their vocables:
Our spiders are both naked and rhetorical.

III

Soliloquy at Nightfall in the Mayflower Hotel

Six Sonnets on Sex and Death

1

Presentiments of chaos in the telephone
alerted his left ear. He strode
over music till he found a road
angled into the fissures of a bone

—elk's bone or caribou? O Wapiti!
The Rockies with their pressure-cooker lids
were fuming when he caught up with the kids
and Mom, all rouged and wizened with graffiti.

"I once had such a tuft of names," he cried,
"a scalp of alphabets, a register
of private pronouns for my personal use!
My fingerprints keep shifting with the tide.
The droll tabloids bandy my moniker
and press me, like a turnip, for my juice."

2

They pressed him like a turnip for his juice
which masqueraded as a precious oil.
He sweated like a basted Christmas goose.
His melancholy simmered at a boil.

They sent a dancer with red razor shoes
to trot the cha-cha on his lollipop.
They sent a leper with the evening news.
He bled laboriously but begged, *Don't stop!*

This was the pietà of vacant laps,
a Golgotha of sparsely furnished rooms.
He knew the scourges of the evening stoops,
the washrag of Veronica, the sad bazooms
of Magdelenian mourners. He knew death
in every snippet of his metered breath.

3

In every snippet of his metered breath
Pleasure erected its revival tent.
Evangelists of pleasure with a wreath
of jism on their zippers would invent
cloud-copulations, cunnilingual caves,
tumescent glaciers of abiding moan,
hollows of labial comes and wallow-slaves
lathered with a lubricated groan;
orgasm-amazons with tidal spasms
slathered his lollipop with lizard tongues,
clammied his gumdrops in their sphagnum chasms
and whinnied as he wobbled on their gongs.
His dong was gorged with all their ambergris
and slithered like a walrus into bliss.

4

He slithered like a walrus into bliss
of nullity, the vacant and the void.
His all-day sucker fluttered for a kiss
but lovely nothingness was unalloyed.
Neuterness annulled his jolly knot.
The vain inane inoculated all
his tousles of temptation with a shot
and left him shipwrecked in a shopping mall
for body parts, the salvage and the wreck
of bartered bladderstones and stale catarrh.
A salesman with a demonstration dick
softsoaped him with a human-skin cigar.
All I'm looking for (he whined) *is a new scar!*
A busker twanged and picked his blue sitar.

5

A busker twanged and picked his blue sitar.
A melancholy baby in a pram
Barfed a gout of frothy, fragrant scum.
A dachshund lapped it while a falling star

Augured inflation and the start of war.
He wondered whether chaos would have come
in any case. His testicles felt numb.
His rectum itched and tingled like a sore.

Mortality was frisky in the lines
of telephones where drowsy mourning doves
felt final conversations in their claws
transmitted in designer valentines.

O deliquescence of our quartz-like loves!
His heartbeat hovered in two grimy paws.

6

His heartbeat hovered in two grimy paws.
He learned the sadness of quotidian
utensils, learned the glum obsidian
of office lobbies with their cattelyas
and cycads, learned to wind the gauze
of hypochondria around his median;
learned banks of exile quite Ovidian.
Only the Eberhart Faber pencils gave him pause:

cylindrical and golden as a happiness,
solar-yellow, tallow-fluted, saffron-bold.
O happiness remembered in distress!
O vaporous savor of some vanished gold!

Unwritten scripts lay tacit in their tips.
Erasers stiff as nipples rubbed his lips.

Microcosm

The proboscis of the drab gray flea
Is mirrored in the majesty
Of the elephant's articulated trunk. There's a sea
In the bed-mite's dim, orbicular eye
Pinnacles crinkle when the mountain-winged, shy
Moth wakes up and stretches for the night.
Katydids enact the richly patterned light
Of galaxies in their chirped and frangible notes.
The smallest beings harbour a universe
Of telescoped similitudes. Even those Rocky Mountain goats
Mimic Alpha Centauri in rectangular irises
Of cinnabar-splotched gold. Inert viruses
Replicate the static of red-shifted, still chthonic
Cosmoi. Terse
As the listened brilliance of the pulsar's bloom
The violaceous mildew in the corner room
Proliferates in Mendelian exuberance.
There are double stars in the eyes of cyclonic
Spuds shovelled and spaded up. The dance
Of Shiva is a cobble-soled affair,
—hobnails and flapping slippers on the disreputable stair.
Yggdrasils
Germinate on Wal-Mart windowsills.

My Grandfather's Pocket Watch

1

The filigreed watch-case clicks open and inside
I find time's intimate machinery:
The interlocking wheels' circumference,
The pintoothed sprockets that still coincide,
Even though the little self-important melody
That marked the subdivisions of the hour
Is busted now and mute.
Desolate of consequence,
The pocket watch's innards look like our
Old diagrams of the Ptolemaic heavens
With epicyclical and sweet-greased spheres
—except that *Made in U.S.A.* appears
etched on a satiny spring,
and *George Evans*
& Son, New York, glints up from another.

2

A second-hand still whiskers the watch's face
And staggers when I shake it in my fist.

The dark dials mutter like two summer bees
Imprisoned in petals and I feel them beat

—the ratchet of a rope let down into a well:
breathless and staccato and discrete—

each instant demarcated by a brittle click
that falters and then halts until it's shook.

The watch is dove and pearl and velveteen
Behind the dour digits of its face

Like hand-embroidered textiles or the stuffs
William Morris designed: vine-tangled arabesques

Emblematic of luxuriance and rich
Tissues drawn from some profounder life.

I twist the stem and listen for the tick
Till a tiny, startled, hurrying succession

Of twig-snapped seconds comes tiptapping out.
Each soft click is a comfort to my touch.

Against Memorials

We will crevice all their names
in fingertip niches of a wall,
the way that pious Jews
tucked names and messages,
the smallest written slip
bearing or alluding to
the name of God
into genizas or
between the stones
of the massive grass-sprigged masonry
of the wall of lamentation and of memory.

We're tired of the blaze of the monuments.
Even as children in the civic sun
we had no patience with memorials.
Better to keep their memories the way
mothers slip mementos,
most cherished because simplest, most quotidian
—a birthday card, a button, or a leaf—
into the shyest alcove of a drawer.
The smallest are the strongest monuments.

For us let recollection live
in the blue thistle of roadsides, in
the dandelions' puffed domes. In swiftness
of squill, acknowledgement. Memorial, heart's
ease, in the columns of the clover, in
the burdock's spurs.

Soliloquy at Nightfall in the Mayflower Hotel
(Jacksonville, Florida, Winter 1937)

> "In each of us, I said to myself, there is a place remote and islanded, and given to endless regret or secret happiness; we are each the uncompanioned hermit and recluse of an hour or a day; we understand our fellows of the cell to whatever age of history they may belong."
>
> —Sarah Orne Jewett, *The Country of the Pointed Firs*

Even here, in Jacksonville, in the gritty twilight
of a decaying city, in the Mayflower Hotel
—it's known better days, believe you me—if a
lover came climbing up the third-floor stairs,
I'd anoint my throat and shoulders as I heard his steps,
as I heard him padding down the tatty carpet of the corridor
I'd be dabbing little droplets of rare scent across my skin,
and as he tapped O how discreetly he would tap!
the smell of my skin would waft all through my room
and if I let him in—you notice I say *if*—
my perfume would entwine him all around
and in those twinking lights from the muddy stream
I'd see the dark flecks of his pupils gleam.
I have seen men's faces smitten with desire.
I have seen men's faces tauten and grow young
and their desire excited me, I felt oh I felt riverine,
not like the shabby St. John's but a musky sweet
river of paradise racing from the clouds—

BANG BANG BANG—"It's Missus Huey, dear!"
Shattered my daydream, shattered it to bits . . .
GO AWAY! GO AWAY! But will she hear me?
"Now, dear Virginia, I don't like to think of you
all alone at evening in this dreary lodging house!"

I hear her flutey voice, I imagine her dowdy hat,
and cruel fantasies begin to work in me. I see
Mrs. Huey bending over while behind her, unbeknownst
to her, some deep-sea creature crawls to ravish her.
A squid or a lobster. Yes, a giant spiny lobster
with an immense pink *membrum virile* . . .

"DEAR DEAR! OPEN THIS DOOR RIGHT NOW, YOU HEAR?"
The lobster mounts her from behind. She shrieks.
Its claws shred her panties—that cheap McCrory's brand!
—its antennae fondle her pendulous . . . its mandibles
nibble at her blushing . . . at her flushed and moistened . . .
she is screaming but her screams subside in moans,
the lobster has splayed her on the corridor, he is about to
ravish Mrs. Huey, his member is throbbing with a tidal
pulse, coarse-veined, a rosy prong, she sighs . . .

Did I take my Feenamint? Indigestion! Again!
That hog-jowl! GO
AWAY! "Now, my dear," her lobster-pleasured voice
begins again (I hear her ravisher scuttling down the stairs),
"I am just going to *encamp* like an A-rab
at your doorway, till you let me in, you hear?"

May Beelzebub and all his crew skewer and
Baste your chops, you meddling nincompoop!

But cheerily I sing through the bolted door:
"O dear Mrs. Huey, how divinely kind of you! Last night
was a horror for me. Head shuddering, limbs buzzing, I had
the megrims, couldn't sleep, my bowels were churning, I must
have reacted to some bean soup I had at that Spanish restaurant . . . "
"You went to that *dago* place?" Mrs. Huey wails. As though they
weren't as white, or to use her word, as *Aryan*, as she.
Oh why doesn't Mr. Underwood come knocking at my door
instead of this common hoyden?

When Mr. Underwood
stopped at my table the other evening, while Mrs. Huey
fumed, I could see that he was a man of parts, one of the old
school, dapper, splashed with some fine cologne,
a small half-opening gardenia in his buttonhole
and the loveliest pair of fawn gloves, spats, a crisp
brimmed hat, and that divinely double-breasted suit
that showed his manly form to full advantage . . .

Papa would have approved of Mr. Underwood,
I do believe. I think the Huey woman's gone at last,
—she has despaired of her quarry! Back to Opportunity
School for her, where the grateful pickaninnies
positively sop up her largesse. Faughgh!!!

The lights are winking still and I feel moved to declaim
those verses Ellen C. Howarth once penned for me:

Where is the heart that doth not keep
within its inmost core,
Some fond remembrance hidden deep
of days that are no more?

Of course, Ellen was a fool. Where *is* the heart, indeed?
What claptrap! The core of my heart was shattered as a child
and I am perfectly happy to hide those days that are no more
as deeply as I can. The core of my heart! It was my destiny
to be—how say it?—*uncored*, like the last apple in the bin
that sucks all its own fading sweetnesses within,
—to have been *overlooked*, all my life long. That was my
destiny. To be Daddy's favorite daughter all my life,
and Daddy long dead and gone.

Now it is star-rise I remember how the chime
of the doorbell signaled us to file
into the parlor where shy gentlemen
were lined in muster for our fierce Papa.
In our "at homes," on summer nights,
Papa would strut, parade himself, declaim
"The Bard" while I and my three sisters writhed.

Who is it NOW? I am ill, do you hear, I cannot
receive tonight, I am doing poorly (Where *is* that
Feenamint?) What do you say? Amelia Earhart
is still missing? Is that Pastor Butts? (Old Pastor
Lard-Butts, I call him, with his dirty monkey
collar turned around!) Amelia Who?
(As though I cared!)

O my dear Amelia,
I've explored worse coastlines sitting here at night
in the Mayflower Hotel with the river down below
than all the shores your airplane could encounter . . .
and I have been lost for decades now, Amelia,
the search parties have given up, the rescuers have
forgotten, the bloodhounds have lost the trace
and laid their muzzles on their weary paws . . . !)

"Oh, is it Mr. Underwood? My dear, a moment please!"
I'll wear *My Sin* and slip my peignoir on,
I'll fluff my permanent and use some rouge . . .
"What? You'll call again? But no. . . Give me a minute, hear?"
That is the sound I associate with grief:
the sound of footsteps receding down a hall,
the diminishing sound of shoe soles on a rug
scff scff scfff and then no more no more nothing at all
silence of a corridor in an old woman's hotel . . .

"Years are the milestones that tell us
the distance we have traveled." So it said in my gold-
clasped diary, the one Mama gave me years ago.
I am almost seventy and I have traveled hardly at all,
my milestones must be mile-pebbles, or maybe, inch-
stones. Yes, I have walked and walked, I have even run,
and I find myself now, here, as though I hadn't begun
at all, and the road stretched out before me still,
my father's daughter, still at the starting-line.

But O how terrifying Papa was
in those *days that are no more!*
He was the bramble bush that thorned us in,
the high-topped wall no suitor could surmount.
I used to watch his sideburns wattle as he paced
and plumed himself and trailed his fiery eye
across each trembling suitor's finery
with histrionic hectoring assessor's gaze.
He seemed to price their collars and cravats,
their gloves and the rubbed brass buttons of their cuffs.

Worse, puffing out his iambs, with a scarlet
suffusion of bright blood across both cheeks,
his strict hand lofted, his pinstriped knee thrust forth,
Milmow's occupation gone! he'd roar or then,
hissingly, with daggered fingers, spout
how sharper than a serpent's tooth it is
to have a thankless child!

How could any suitor withstand Papa?
For all of them, poor fops, I felt contempt.
Who of them could muster me and make me feel
known to the very skin of me, as Papa could?

Well, the river is still shining. I can almost hear
laughter in the little flitting lights
that steeple each dark wave. I do not like
the shine of the moon on the windowsill.
I do not like the look or the touch of silver.
Silver has always had for me, since then,
since those *days that are no more,*
an almost sarcastic luster I abhor.
Sitting here in the evening, by myself,
unable to put my hands on a single Feenamint
while my indigestion positively rages,
with neither Mr. Underwood nor even that
impossible woman with the tacky hat,
nor—and I thank the Lord!—that greasy Pastor Butts,
I'll never let the moonlight or the bright
mouth of the river
sweet-talk and swindle me and leave behind
only dry crusts to gnaw my life out on.
The moon can sidle in and do its worst
to prettify my sitting room. I trust
only in darkness that refuses silver.

Lines Written after Reading Thomas à Kempis

Take comfort from your nothingness.
Inconsequence is not futility.
Get pleasure from becoming less.

Such diminution is not mimicry:
the cloud is cloudier than all cloudedness
but gets a pleasure in becoming less.

At night the skin of love becomes a sea
yet takes a comfort from its nothingness
(in consequence is not futility);

a sea that stipples at the cloud's caress
takes pleasure in becoming ever less.
Solace lies in what the lucent sea

gives up by gaining all translucency:
Take comfort from your nothingness,
Get pleasure from becoming less.